MW00897316

the Big Sis

ACTIVITY BOOK

♥ THANK YOU SO MUCH FOR YOUR PURCHASE!
IF YOU ENJOYED THIS BOOK, PLEASE CONSIDER
LEAVING A REVIEW ON AMAZON.
YOU CAN ALSO FIND MORE COOL BOOKS BY
SCANNING THE CODE BELOW!

Dreamy Night Press

This book belongs to big sis:

Little Sibling

Arriving Soon

HELLO THERE! MY NAME IS NALA, AND I AM A PART OF THE BIG SISTERS CLUB. I HEARD YOU ARE GOING TO BE A BIG SISTER, TOO. THAT IS SO EXCITING! AS EXCITING AS IT IS, I ALSO KNOW A CHANGE THIS BIG CAN BE A LITTLE OVERWHELMING. I JUST WANTED TO LET YOU KNOW THAT EVERYTHING WILL TURN OUT GREAT, AND YOUR NEW SIBLING WILL SOON BECOME YOUR NEW FAVORITE PLAYMATE! THIS BOOK IS FOR YOU TO DO WHILE YOU WAIT FOR THE BABY TO ARRIVE, OR WHILE MOM IS BUSY WITH BABY. WELCOME TO THE BIG SISTERS CLUB & ENJOY!

-NALA

BIG SISTER

Certificate

this certificate is awarded to:

_____

For Becoming the BEST big sister ever!

Witnesses:

_____

Effective Date:

_____   _____

COUNTING

Count the images & write your answer in the square.

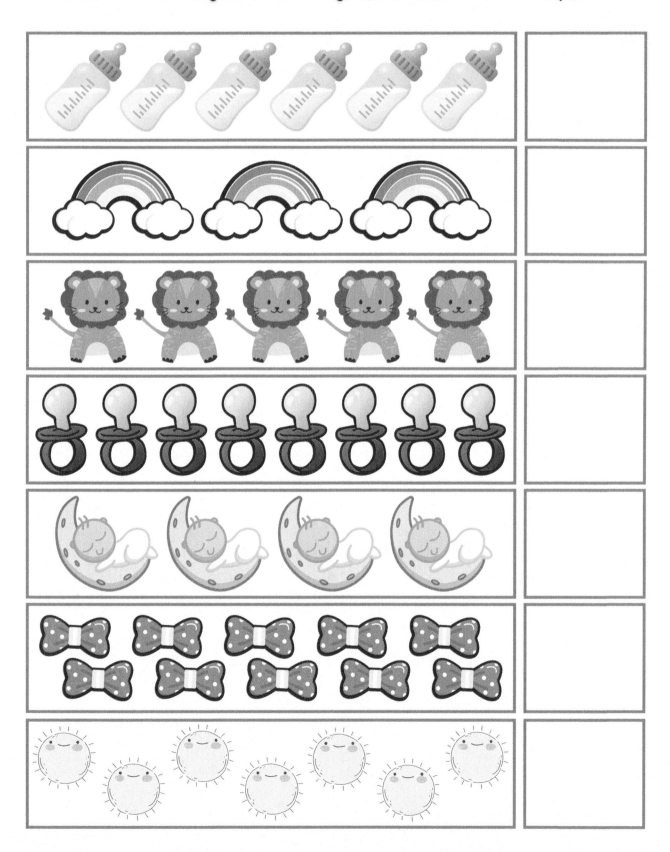

WORD SEARCH

Find and circle the words listed below.

S	I	B	L	I	N	G	S	I	B
I	M	L	Y	C	Z	M	D	H	A
A	F	A	M	I	L	Y	X	W	B
B	X	N	R	P	O	H	D	Q	Y
O	H	K	M	W	V	P	R	U	S
T	I	E	J	A	E	V	M	O	M
T	W	T	Q	B	U	M	Z	I	B
L	F	Q	S	I	S	T	E	R	D
E	K	V	D	B	E	Z	W	H	A
S	T	R	O	L	L	E	R	J	D

BABY   BIB   DAD

SISTER   FAMILY   SIBLINGS

LOVE   BLANKET   BOTTLE

STROLLER   MOM

CAN YOU SPOT THE 7 DIFFERENCES IN THE PICTURES BELOW?

GRID ART

Use the grid to help draw the other side.

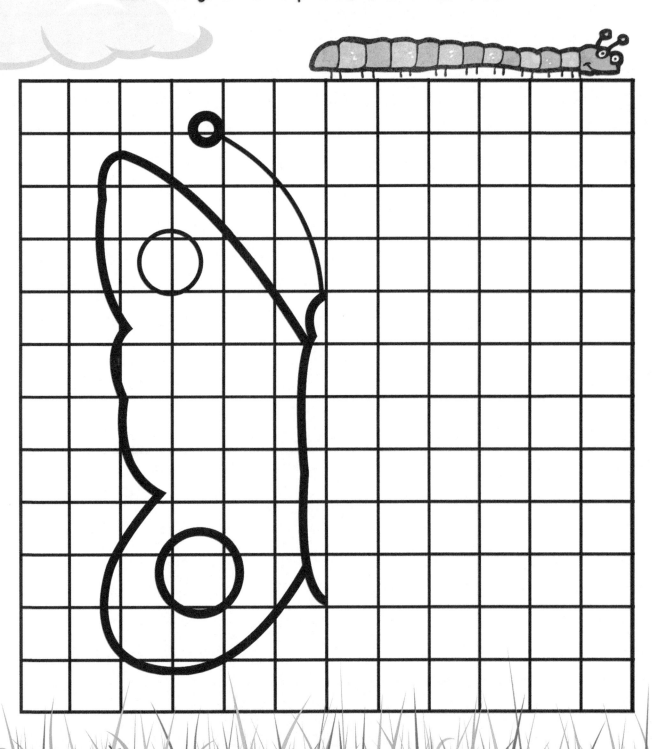

SHADOW MATCHING

Draw a line to connect each baby animal to it's shadow.

CAN YOU SPOT THE 7 DIFFERENCES IN THE PICTURES BELOW?

COUNT & COLOR

Count the buns in the oven. Record your answer below.

How many buns are there? _____

MAZE TIME

Can you help this big sister find the teddy bear?

LET'S GET CREATIVE

Decorate this plant pot for your new brother or sister.

COLOR BY NUMBERS

Color the rainbow according to the chart below.

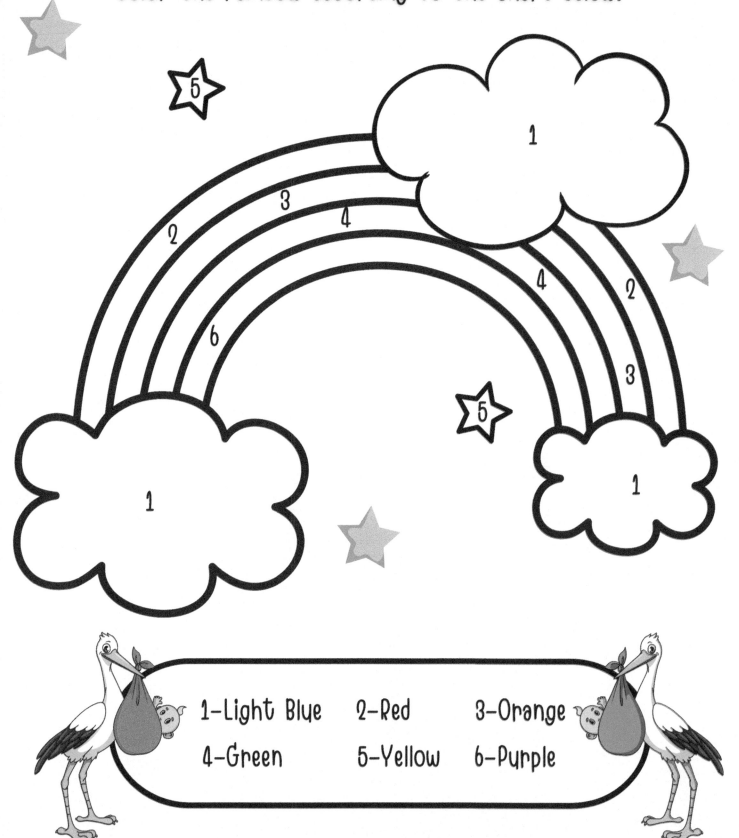

1-Light Blue   2-Red   3-Orange
4-Green   5-Yellow   6-Purple

SPOT THE ODD ONE OUT

Circle the 'odd one out' from each group below.

GRID ART

Use the grid to help draw the other side.

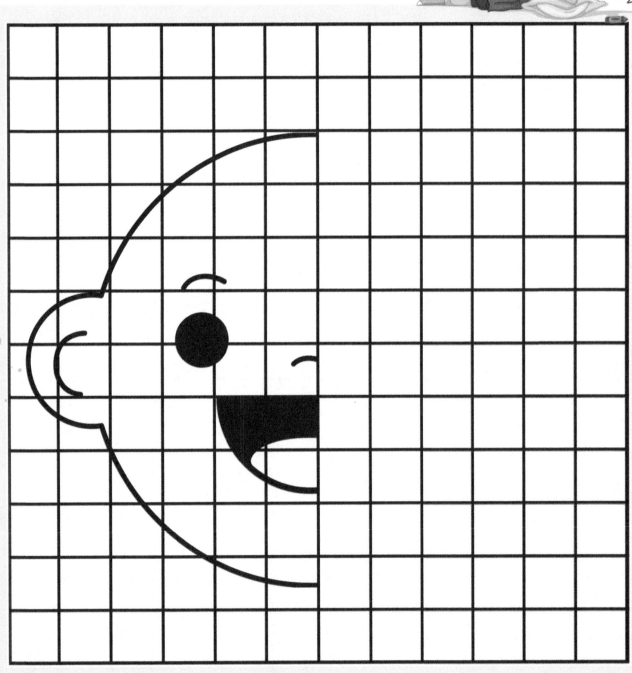

CAN YOU SPOT THE 7 DIFFERENCES IN THE PICTURES BELOW?

COUNTING

Count the images & write your answer in the square.

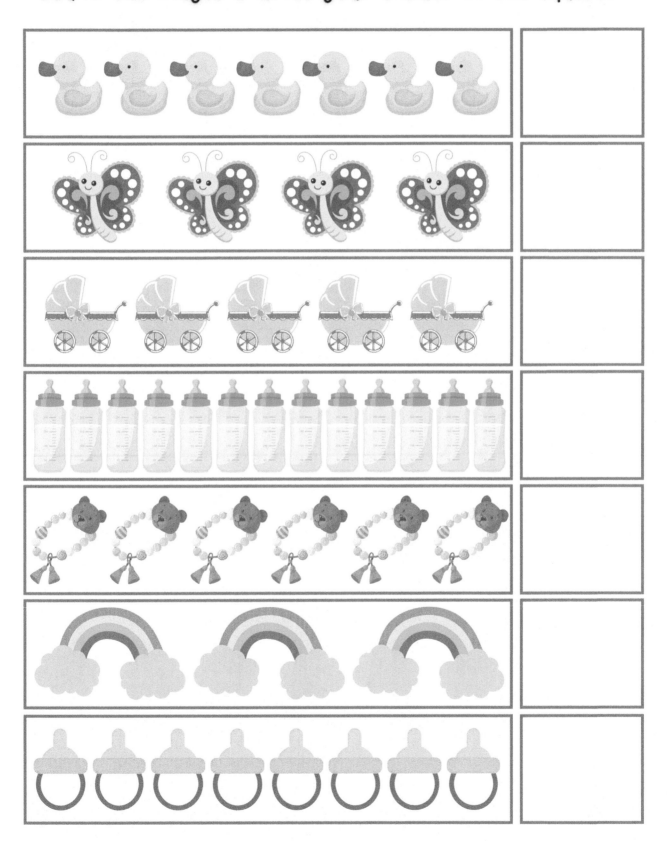

LET'S GET CREATIVE

Decorate these shoes for your new brother or sister.

HOW MANY?

Count how many of each animal you see. Record your answers below.

___ ___ ___ ___ ___ ___ ___ ___

COUNT & COLOR

Count and color the exact number listed.

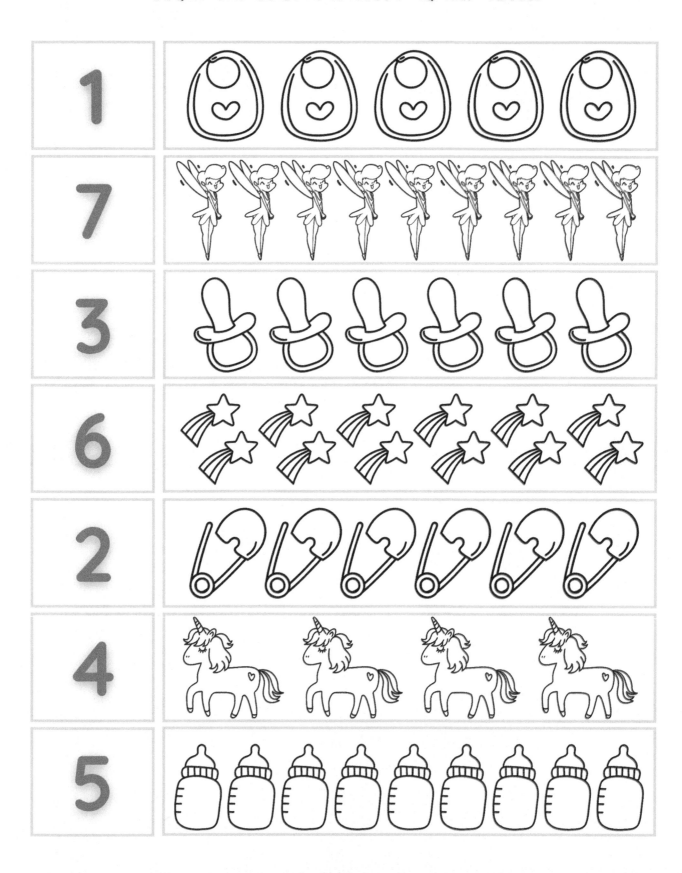

1

7

3

6

2

4

5

COLOR BY NUMBERS

Color the picture according to the chart below.

1-Gray   2-Pink   3-Purple

4-Orange   5-Yellow   6-Blue

CAN YOU SPOT THE 7 DIFFERENCES IN THE PICTURES BELOW?

FILL IN THE BLANK

Fill in the missing letters.

SPOT THE DIFFERENCE

Circle and color the baby that is not like the others.

COUNT & COLOR

Count and color the fireflies in the jar.

How many fireflies do you see? _____

LET'S GET CREATIVE

Color in these cute little critters.

SHADOW MATCHING

Color in the baby toys, then draw a line to it's shadow.

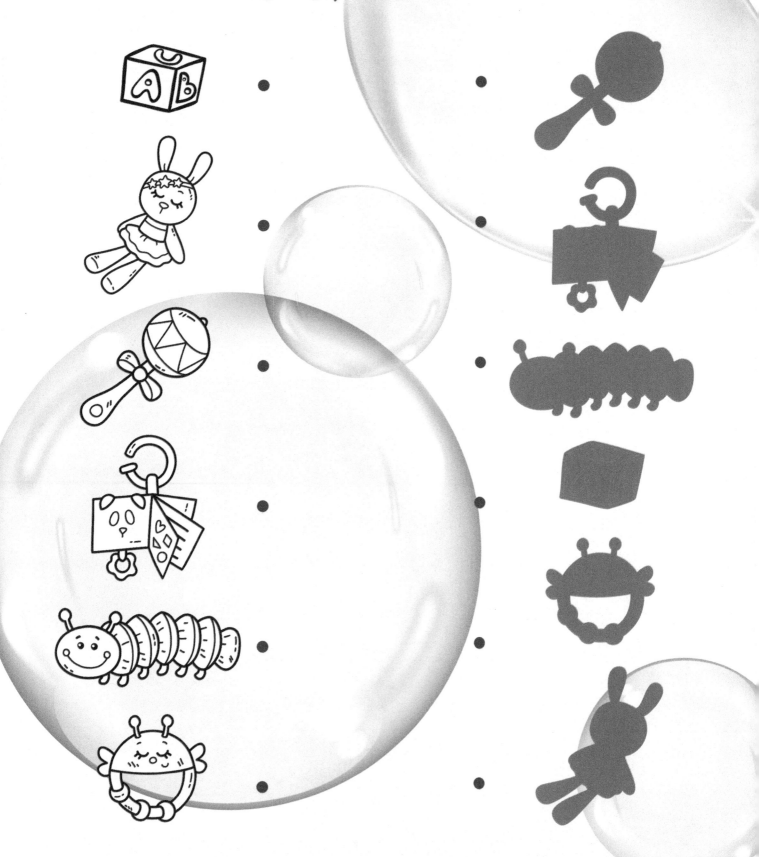

TIC TAC TOE

GRID ART

Use the grid to help draw the other side.

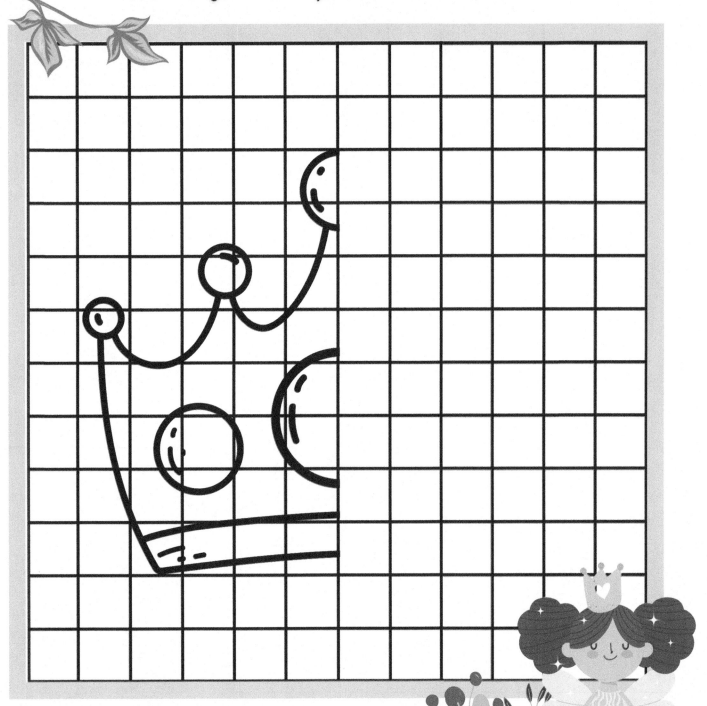

CAN YOU SPOT THE 7 DIFFERENCES IN THE PICTURES BELOW?

MAZE TIME

Can you help the stork deliver the baby home?

CAN YOU SPOT THE 7 DIFFERENCES IN THE PICTURES BELOW?

CHALLENGE
WORD SCRAMBLE

Unscramble the letters. Write the word down & connect to the correct picture.

ETRSIS	SISTER
FYLTTERBU	
EVLO	
RBNIAOW	
KETANBL	
ORBNWEN	
YTEDD RBEA	
TTLRAE	
APPHY	
BRCI	

HANDWRITING PRACTICE

Write a kind letter to your new sibling!

FAVORITE BOOKS

List your favorite books to share with baby.

FIND MORE COLORING BOOKS!

& FREE COLORING PAGES!

HERE!

89086296R00057